SPACE STICKER STORY TIME

FIVE MILE

The Wiggles are getting ready for a
space adventure. Wake up, Lachy!
It is time to go!

Their mission is to collect plant samples from the Space Dome and bring them back to Earth.

Use your flag sticker to complete the picture!

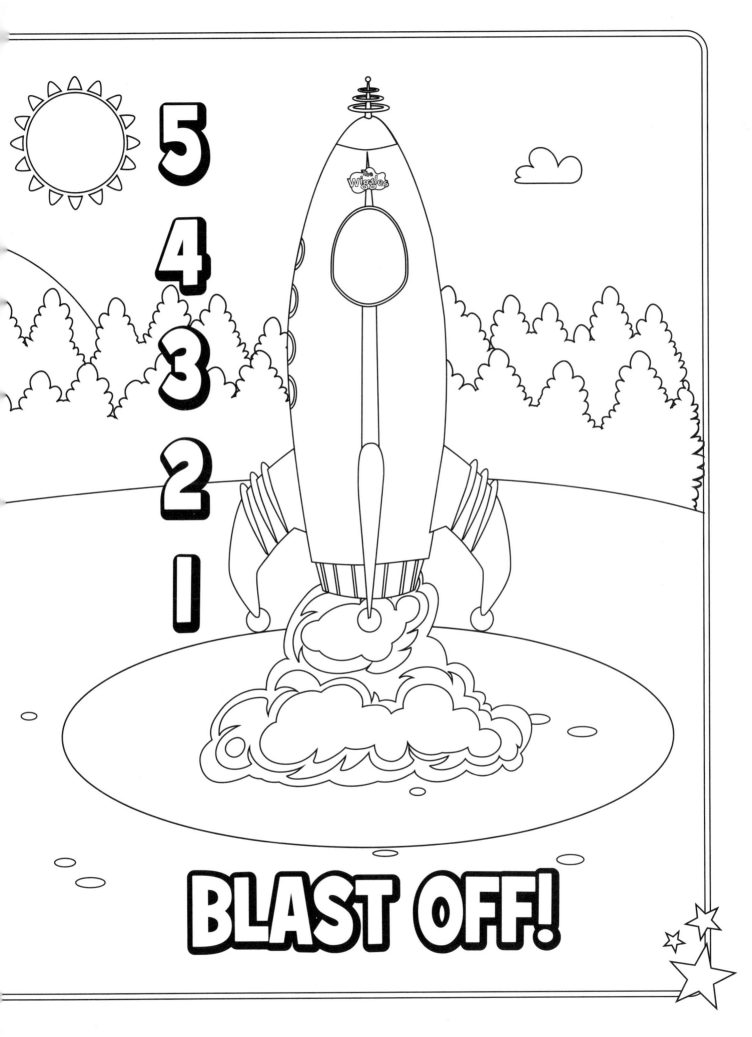

Inside the Big Red Spaceship, The Wiggles can take off their helmets.

To go outside the Big Red Spaceship, they need to put on their helmets. There is no oxygen in space!

The Wiggles cannot wait to step outside and explore the planet.

Use your Lachy sticker to complete the picture!

They get out of the Big Red Spaceship and jump around.

Lachy and Anthony are excited to be off on a space walk!

Use your spaceship sticker to complete the picture!

They have so much fun floating around in space.

Time to jump into the space rover and head to the Space Dome.

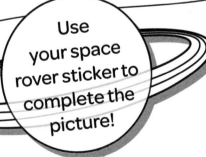

Use your space rover sticker to complete the picture!

The Space Dome is a round building built to be a bit like Earth, but on another planet.

Use your planet stickers to complete the picture!

It has oxygen, water and plants inside.

These are the plants growing inside the Space Dome.

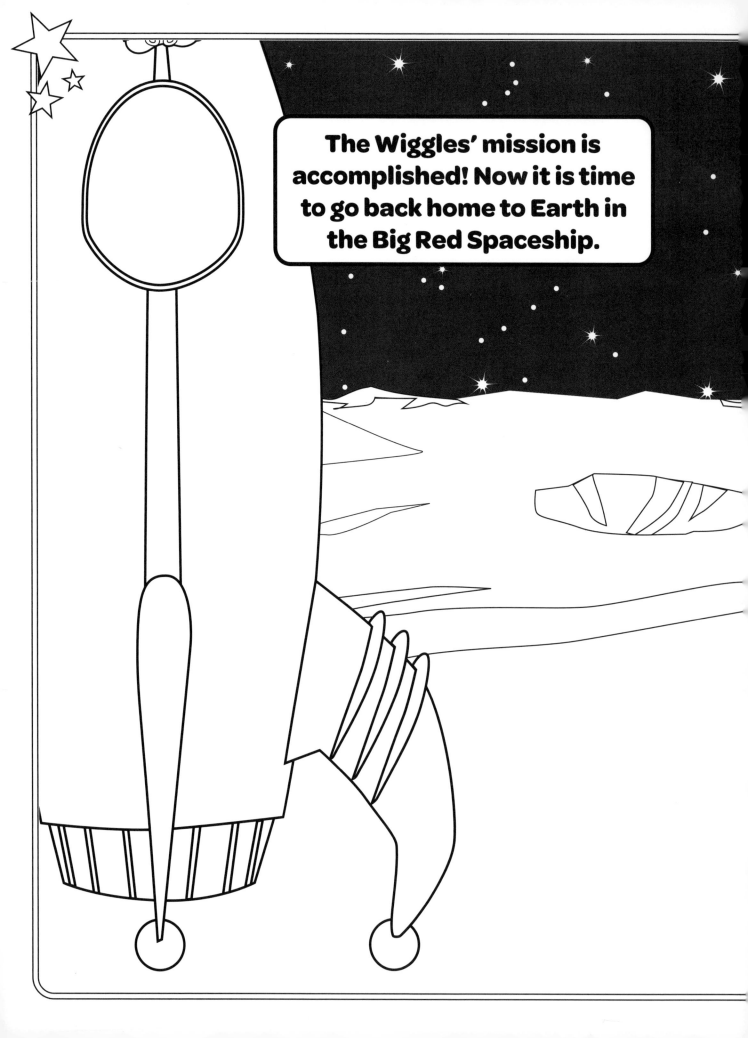

The Wiggles' mission is accomplished! Now it is time to go back home to Earth in the Big Red Spaceship.

Use your Tsehay sticker to complete the picture!

Use your Simon sticker to complete the picture!

It is good to be home.